Crafts from Junk

by Violaine Lamérand

Translated by Cheryl L. Smith

Reading Consultant:
Dr. Robert Miller
Professor of Special Education
Minnesota State University, Mankato

Bridgestone Books
an imprint of Capstone Press
Mankato, Minnesota

Table of contents

words to know

acrylic paint (uh-KRIL-ik PAINT)—a type of paint made from chemicals

punch tool (PUNCH TOOL)—a pointed tool used to poke holes in wood or leather; an awl is a type of punch tool.

raffia (RAH-fee-uh)—the fiber of the raffia palm tree; this strawlike fiber is often used in crafts.

recycle (ree-SYE-kuhl)—to make used items into new products; people can recycle items such as glass, plastic, newspapers, and aluminum cans.

reinforce (ree-in-FORSS)—to make something stronger

Originally published as *Bouts de Ficelle: Récupérer et Créer*, © 1998 Editions Milan.

Bridgestone Books are published by Capstone Press
151 Good Counsel Drive, P.O. Box 669, Mankato, Minnesota 56002
http://www.capstone-press.com

Library of Congress Cataloging-in-Publication Data
Lamérand, Violaine.
    Crafts from junk/by Violaine Lamérand; translated by Cheryl L. Smith.
    p. cm.—(Step by step)
    Includes index.
    Summary: Provides patterns and detailed instructions for thirteen crafts made from junk.
    ISBN 0-7368-1479-5 (hardcover)
    1. Handicraft—Juvenile literature. 2. Recycling (Waste, etc.)–Juvenile literature. [1. Handicraft. 2. Junk. 3. Recycling (Waste)] I. Title. II. Step by step (Mankato, Minn.)
TT160 .L322 2003
745.5--dc21
                                        2002002173

1 2 3 4 5 6 07 06 05 04 03 02

Editor:
Rebecca Glaser

Photographs:
Milan/Dominique Chauvet;
Capstone Press/Gary Sundermeyer

Graphic Design:
Sarbacane

Design Production:
Steve Christensen

Little Tricks

You can collect and recycle many things: cardboard tubes, cereal boxes, egg cartons, and all sizes of shoe boxes. Thoroughly wash and dry milk and juice cartons, and yogurt cups. Make a toolbox to hold your collection (see page 14).

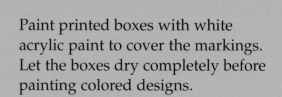

Paint printed boxes with white acrylic paint to cover the markings. Let the boxes dry completely before painting colored designs.

Use double-sided tape to put together plastic materials.

Ask an adult to help you poke a hole in plastic bottle caps. Use a small punch tool or awl. If you do not have these tools, you can use a hammer and nail.

Be Careful!
Ask an adult to use a utility knife to cut corrugated cardboard.

5

Flower Frame

1 Cut the cover off the egg carton. Cut out each egg cup in a flower shape.

3 Glue the flowers around the edge of the cover.

2 Paint the cover. Paint the center of the flowers and then the petals. Let the cover and flowers dry.

4 Tie a knot in the raffia and glue it to the back of the frame for hanging. Place a picture in the frame.

Eggs once came in
wooden boxes called
egg crates. Today, eggs
come in paper cartons
that can be recycled.

Stilts

You Will Need:
- **2 large tin cans**
- **Colored paper**
- **Double-sided tape**
- **Punch tool**
- **2 clothesline cords 60 inches (152 centimeters) long**
- **Scissors**
- **Glue**

2 Ask an adult to make a hole on both sides of the can near the bottom. Run the ends of the clothesline through the holes. Tie a knot inside the can.

3 To decorate the cans, glue pieces of colored paper onto the first strip of colored paper. Change the length of the cords by moving the knots. The stretched cords should reach to your waist.

1 Cut out a strip of colored paper large enough to cover each can. Use double-sided tape to attach the paper to the cans.

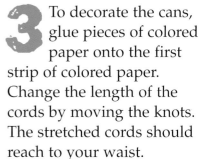

Tin cans are made mostly of steel. A thin coating of tin protects the steel. Both tin and steel can be recycled easily.

9

Mouse Mask

You Will Need:
- Egg carton
- Paint
- Paintbrush
- Clean foam meat tray
- Glue
- Straws
- Stapler

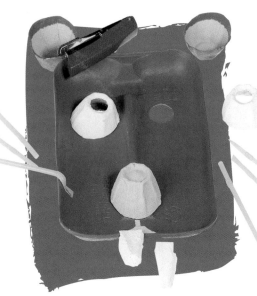

1 Ask an adult to thoroughly wash the foam tray. Cut out six cups from the egg carton. Cut a hole in the middle of two cups to make eyes. Use the others to make two ears, a nose, and two points for the teeth.

2 Paint all the pieces and let them dry.

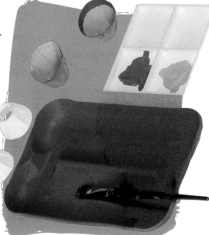

3 Cut two holes 1 ¼ inches (3 centimeters) apart for the eye holes. Glue the eyes, nose, and teeth on the meat tray. Staple the ears and straws on the tray. You can staple on elastic string to wear your mask or you can hold it in front of your face.

Mice have poor eyesight. They use their whiskers to feel where they are going.

11

Topsy-Turvy Heads

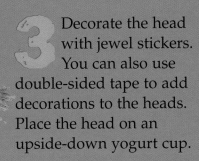

You Will Need:

- 3 small plastic yogurt cups for each head
- Paint
- Paintbrush
- Double-sided tape
- Yarn
- Movable eyes, jewel stickers, or other decorations

1 Paint the yogurt cups. After the cups are dry, put strips of double-sided tape around the edges.

2 Make two tufts of hair from the yarn. Peel off the tape backing and place the hair on each side of the cup. Assemble the two cups, one on top of the other.

3 Decorate the head with jewel stickers. You can also use double-sided tape to add decorations to the heads. Place the head on an upside-down yogurt cup.

You can make a game from your topsy-turvy heads. Glue upside-down yogurt cups to a piece of cardboard. Set the heads on the upside-down cups. Throw a foam rubber ball at the heads to knock them over. See who can knock down the most with one toss.

13

Toolbox

You Will Need:
- Shoe box
- 4 brass fasteners
- Construction paper
- White glue
- Paintbrush

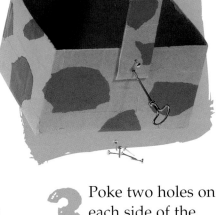

2 Fold the band to the same width as the box. This band will make the handle. Tear pieces of construction paper and glue them to the handle and the box. Protect the box and handle with a coat of white glue. It will dry clear.

3 Poke two holes on each side of the handle and the box. Attach the handle to the box with brass fasteners.

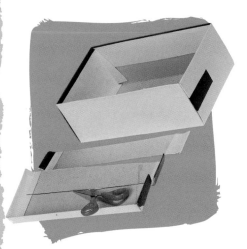

1 Cut out two matching strips from the length of the shoe box cover. Glue one on top of the other to make a strong band.

Cardboard boxes can be recycled. Using recycled cardboard to make new cardboard takes 25 percent less energy than using new wood fiber.

15

Post Office

You Will Need:

- Large cardboard box
- Utility knife
- Glue
- Clothespins
- Paint
- Paintbrush
- Punch tool
- Thin string
- Two juice cartons
- 8 empty matchboxes
- 8 brass fasteners

1 Ask an adult to cut out three sides of a window from the box. Fold the cut out part in half to make a shelf. Glue two halves together. Use clothespins to hold the shelf while it dries. The shelf forms the post office counter.

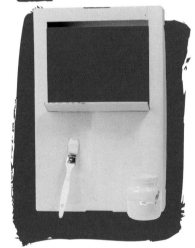

2 Paint the box on all sides.

4 Cut two juice cartons in half. Glue the bottom of one juice carton in the left corner. Glue the bottom of the other one in the right corner. Glue the matchboxes to the juice cartons.

3 Make holes in the top and bottom of the box and on the shelf. Thread string through the holes on the shelf. Knot the string on both sides of the shelf. Thread the string through the holes on the top and bottom of the box. Tie knots on the back of the box to hold the string.

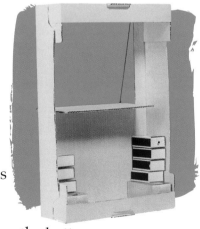

This post office can become a small puppet theater.

You can collect stamps from letters you receive. To remove a stamp from an envelope, soak it in water in a shallow dish. When the stamp comes off the paper, place the stamp on a piece of newspaper. After the stamp is dry, peel it carefully from the newspaper.

5 Put a brass fastener on the front of each matchbox for a drawer handle. Ask an adult to cut a mail slot under the shelf. Glue a small box under the mail slot. Paint the drawers.

Stick Drum

You Will Need:
- Round wooden craft box
- Scissors
- Stick
- Glue
- String
- 2 beads
- Stapler
- Colored paper

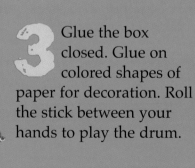

2 Glue the stick into the cover. String each bead on a piece of string 4 inches (10 centimeters) long. Make a knot at the end of each string and staple the strings to the side of the box.

3 Glue the box closed. Glue on colored shapes of paper for decoration. Roll the stick between your hands to play the drum.

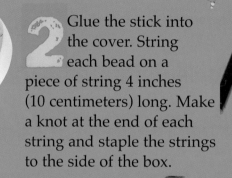

1 Cut out one square from the edge of the box. Cut out a square the same size from the cover.

Many people around the world use stick drums. They may make them by stretching animal skins over two open gourds back to back. Gourds are dried, hollow shells of fruit.

19

Cat and Mouse Game

You Will Need:

- Cardboard pizza box
- Scissors
- 4 plastic yogurt cups
- Double-sided tape
- Paint
- Paintbrush
- Black felt-tip pen
- 4 Styrofoam balls
- Yarn
- Straws

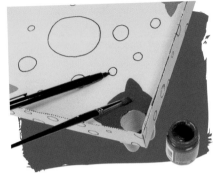

1 Cut off the cover of the pizza box. Staple the corners of the box. Trace a circle in each corner. Poke the scissors in the middle and cut out a star.

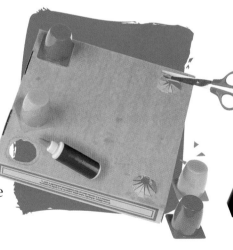

2 Cut off the points of the stars to make circles. Attach a yogurt cup under each hole with double-sided tape.

3 Paint the box yellow. When it is dry, draw circles to make it look like Swiss cheese. Paint a cat face in each corner. The holes will be the cats' mouths.

4 Paint Styrofoam balls the same colors as the cats. The balls will be the mice. Glue a bit of yarn to the mice to make tails. Draw a face on the mice with a felt-tip pen.

Blow into the straws to push the mice around the board. Try to get the mice into the same color cat. You can play by yourself or with as many as four people.

21

Racing cars

1 Make slits on both ends of the tube. Cut a circle for the driver in the middle of the tube.

2 Glue the slits together with one on top of the other. Cut out a rectangle of cardboard the length of the tube. The ridges should run across the short side of the rectangle. Slide two pieces of wooden skewers into the ridges of the cardboard to make axles.

3 Glue the cardboard rectangle to the bottom of the tube. Cut out four mudguards from the cardboard. Bend them and glue them to the tube above the wheel axles. Poke a hole in each bottle cap.

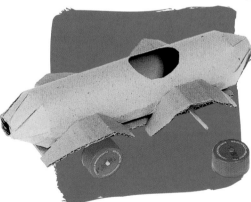

4 Put the bottle caps on the axles. Paint the car as you like. Place a plastic egg with a painted face into the car as a driver.

22

Top fuel dragsters are the fastest type of racecar. They can reach speeds of more than 300 miles (483 kilometers) per hour. They use the same type of fuel as some rockets.

23

Rockets

2 From other tubes, cut out fins and glue them to the rocket. Cut out rectangles and put glue on them. Then roll them up to make tubes. Use clothespins to hold them while they dry. The tubes are rocket boosters.

3 Cut slits in the top of the cardboard tube. Glue the slits together with one on top of the other to make the rocket pointed. Glue the rocket boosters next to the fins. Paint the rocket.

1 Cut your tubes in different lengths. Cut out a part of the bottom on each side to make the bottom of the rocket.

24

Rocket boosters are small rockets attached to a larger rocket to give it extra power.

Airplanes

You Will Need:

- Cardboard tube
- Scissors
- 6 corks
- Corrugated cardboard
- Glue
- Ice cream stick
- Hammer and nail
- Paint
- Paintbrush

3 Cut pieces from the cardboard. Make two wings, one tail piece, and one tail fin. Make a slit in the fin and bend it so it will stand up. Glue the tube to the middle of one wing. Glue the corks at each end of the wings. Glue the other wing to the top.

1 Cut little slits in both ends of the tube to form strips. Cut a hole in the middle of the tube.

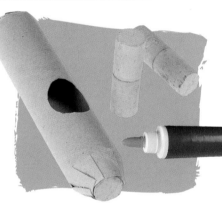

2 Put a cork inside one end and glue the strips to it. On the other end, glue the strips together. Glue two corks together end to end. Then glue two more.

4 Glue the tail piece to the bottom of the plane and the tail fin to the top of the airplane. Gently pound the nail into the ice cream stick. Then push the nail into the cork to attach the stick. Cut two slices of cork and glue these on for landing gear. Paint the airplane.

In the early 1900s, people called barnstormers did a trick called wing walking. They walked out on the wing while the plane was in the air.

Somersaulting Elves

You Will Need:

- **Plastic eggs**
- **Large marbles**
- **Felt**
- **Scissors**
- **Double-sided tape**

3 Put double-sided tape around the middle of the egg. Attach it to the felt body so part of the egg sticks out to make a head. Stick double-sided tape around the body. Put the hands and the feet on top of the tape.

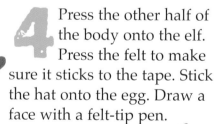

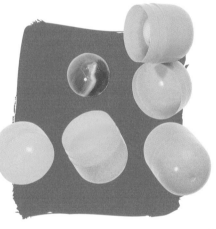

2 Cut two 3-inch (8-centimeter) squares of felt. Cut out the sides to make arms. Cut out a hat, two hands, and two feet from a different color of felt.

4 Press the other half of the body onto the elf. Press the felt to make sure it sticks to the tape. Stick the hat onto the egg. Draw a face with a felt-tip pen.

1 Put a large marble in each egg.

Elves are characters from European folktales. In most stories, elves are tiny people who enjoy singing and dancing.

Doll cradle

You Will Need:

- Large cardboard box
- Small cardboard box
- Utility knife
- Glue
- Acrylic paint
- Paintbrush
- Stickers
- Rectangular piece of cloth, about the size of a kitchen towel
- Ribbon

1 On the large box, trace the shape of the end of the small box. Add a half circle to the top. Ask an adult to cut out the shape with a utility knife. Trace this shape on the rest of the large box and have an adult cut it out.

2 Glue the cut-out shapes to each end of the small box. Let them dry completely.

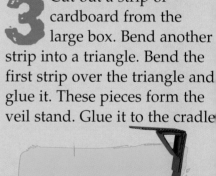

3 Cut out a strip of cardboard from the large box. Bend another strip into a triangle. Bend the first strip over the triangle and glue it. These pieces form the veil stand. Glue it to the cradle.

4 Paint the cradle first with white acrylic paint. When it dries, paint it with colored paint. You can decorate it with stickers.

5 Tie a ribbon in the middle of the cloth and place the veil on its holder. You can also make a mattress and pillow for your cradle.

index